PLAYGROUND SAFETY

by Emma Bassier

Cody Koala

An Imprint of Pop!
popbooksonline.com

abdobooks.com

Published by Pop!, a division of ABDO, PO Box 398166, Minneapolis, Minnesota 55439. Copyright © 2021 by POP, LLC. International copyrights reserved in all countries. No part of this book may be reproduced in any form without written permission from the publisher. Pop!™ is a trademark and logo of POP, LLC.

Printed in the United States of America, North Mankato, Minnesota

052020
092020

♻ **THIS BOOK CONTAINS RECYCLED MATERIALS**

Cover Photo: iStockphoto
Interior Photos: iStockphoto, 1, 5 (top), 5 (bottom left), 5 (bottom right), 8, 11 (top), 11 (bottom left), 12, 14 (top left), 14 (top right), 14 (bottom left), 14 (bottom right), 17, 18, 21; Shutterstock Images, 7, 11 (bottom right)

Editor: Connor Stratton
Series Designer: Christine Ha

Library of Congress Control Number: 2019954993

Publisher's Cataloging-In-Publication Data

Names: Bassier, Emma, author.
Title: Playground safety / by Emma Bassier
Description: Minneapolis, Minnesota : POP!, 2021 | Series: Safety for kids | Includes online resources and index
Identifiers: ISBN 9781532167553 (lib. bdg.) | ISBN 9781532168659 (ebook)
Subjects: LCSH: Playgrounds--Safety measures--Juvenile literature. | Playgrounds--Juvenile literature. | Play--Social aspects--Juvenile literature. | Safety education--Juvenile literature. | Accidents-- Prevention--Juvenile literature.
Classification: DDC 796.068--dc23

Hello! My name is

Cody Koala

Pop open this book and you'll find QR codes like this one, loaded with information, so you can learn even more!

Scan this code* and others like it while you read, or visit the website below to make this book pop.

popbooksonline.com/playground-safety

*Scanning QR codes requires a web-enabled smart device with a QR code reader app and a camera.

Table of Contents

Chapter 1
Jumping and Climbing. . . . 4

Chapter 2
Before Playing. 6

Chapter 3
Following the Rules 10

Chapter 4
Playing Safe. 16

Making Connections 22
Glossary. 23
Index 24
Online Resources 24

Chapter 1

Jumping and Climbing

Miguel reaches the top of a climbing area. Before jumping, he looks at the ground. He makes sure no one is under him. That helps everyone stay safe.

Watch a video here!

Chapter 2

Before Playing

Before you play, make sure an adult is with you. Adults can help if someone gets hurt. Leave your belongings out of the play area. Those items can trip people.

Learn more here!

Touch metal swings and slides before using them. If the **equipment** is hot, it's not safe to use.

Don't run or play on wet equipment. Rain can make playgrounds **slippery**.

> Metal that is too hot can burn people's skin.

Chapter 3

Following the Rules

Playground rules help people stay safe and have fun. Take turns while playing. Don't push or be **rough** with others.

Complete an activity here!

Use the playground's **equipment** how it is meant to be used. Slide down slides feetfirst. On a seesaw, sit facing the other person. Hold on while it moves. Don't climb the seesaw or try to stand in the middle.

Rules for Playground Equipment

Slide

sit down, go feetfirst

Swings

sit, hold on, don't jump off

Merry-go-round

sit, hold on,
don't crowd

Seesaw

face forward, hold on,
don't climb in the middle

Make sure you don't **crowd** a merry-go-round. Sit and hold on to the bars while it spins.

Sit on swings instead of standing or kneeling. Hold the chains. And don't jump off.

Chapter 4

Playing Safe

Stay where an adult can see you. Tell someone if you go to the bathroom. Also, don't talk to **strangers**. If you feel scared, walk away. You can kick and scream for help.

Learn more here!

17

Always look where you are going. You could trip on rocks or bumpy ground. Look around before sliding or swinging. Make sure other kids aren't in the way.

Swings are made to hold one person at a time.

Bend your knees when jumping off monkey bars or other **equipment**. That will help you land without falling. Playing carefully makes sure everyone is safe and has fun.

Making Connections

Text-to-Self

What is your favorite place to play? What do you like about it?

Text-to-Text

Have you read other books about safety tips? How were those safety tips similar to or different from the tips described in this book?

Text-to-World

Some playgrounds are indoors. Others are outside. What extra steps should a person do at an outdoor playground to stay safe?

Glossary

crowd – to sit or stand close to lots of other people in one place.

equipment – poles, tunnels, stairs, platforms, and other parts of a playground.

rough – acting in an out-of-control way that can cause harm to others.

slippery – when something is so smooth or wet that it is hard to walk on or hold.

stranger – someone that a person does not know.

Index

adults, 6, 16

climbing areas, 4

merry-go-rounds, 14, 15

monkey bars, 20

seesaws, 13, 14

slides, 9, 13, 14

strangers, 16

swings, 9, 14, 15, 19

Online Resources

popbooksonline.com

Thanks for reading this Cody Koala book!

Scan this code* and others like it in this book, or visit the website below to make this book pop!

popbooksonline.com/playground-safety

*Scanning QR codes requires a web-enabled smart device with a QR code reader app and a camera.